13724

THE SIKH WORLD

Daljit Singh and Angela Smith

Silver Burdett Company
Morristown, New Jersey

Editor
Peter Harrison
Managing Editor
Belinda Hollyer
Factual Consultant
W. Owen Cole
Design
Sally Boothroyd
Picture Research
Caroline Mitchell
Production
Rosemary Bishop

We are grateful for the assistance of Mrs. Raj
Kaur Singh; Martin Palmer and colleagues at
ICOREC; and the management committee of
Siri Guru Nanak Ninakar gurdwara,
Manchester.

First published in Great Britain in 1985
by Macdonald & Company (Publishers) Ltd
London and Sydney
A member of BPCC plc

Adapted and published in the
United States in 1985 by
Silver Burdett Company,
Morristown, New Jersey

Cover picture: Visitors, barefoot out of
respect, approach the Golden Temple at
Amritsar.

Endpapers: Sikhs bathing and drinking
before entering the gurdwara in Anandpur.

Title page: Printing cloth by hand using
vegetable dyes, a traditional skill in the
Punjab.

Contents page: A Sikh mother and child
attending a Sikh gathering together.

Macdonald & Co. (Publishers) Ltd.
Maxwell House
74 Worship Street
London EC2A 2EN

**Library of Congress Cataloging in
Publication Data**
Daljeet Singh.
 The Sikh world.
 (Religions of the world)
 Bibliography: p.
 Includes index.
 Summary: Describes the origin, beliefs,
place of worship, holy book, ceremonies,
festivals, and special signs of the Sikh faith.
 1. Sikhism – Juvenile literature.
 [1. Sikhism]
I. Smith, Angela. II. Title. III. Series.
BL2018.D336 1985   294.6   85–61673
ISBN 0–382–09159–0
ISBN 0–382–09158–2 (Lib. bdg.)

Contents

Who are the Sikhs?

The Sikhs are people who follow the teachings of ten leaders, whom they call Gurus. All the Gurus lived between 1469 and 1708, in the part of northern India called the Punjab.

The first Guru was born in 1469. The main religions in India at that time were Hinduism and Islam. Members of these two religions followed practices which Guru Nanak rejected. Muslims (followers of Islam) and Hindus saw God in different ways. Hindus also divided people into different groups, called castes, according to what family they were born into; Muslims did not. Some 17th century Indian rulers also used their power to force Hindus into becoming Muslims.

Joining and dividing
Despite all this, the ten Gurus felt that the two religions could and should learn to respect one another. They looked for common ground which would bring the two groups together, and found a different way of thinking about religion.

Over the centuries the Gurus guided the Sikh religion as it grew in numbers and strength in India, but by 1947 the Punjab, the birthplace of Sikhism, was divided between India and Pakistan. Many Sikhs who had lived in what became Pakistan found themselves homeless, so they went to join other Sikhs who had settled in different countries. Sikhs now live in many parts of the world, including

Below: Although most Sikhs come from Indian families, people from other backgrounds have become Sikhs, like this American woman reading to a friend's child.

Canada, the United States of America, Kenya and Germany, but most of the Sikhs outside India live in Britain.

Life and dress

Sikhs do a variety of jobs in the countries where they now live. Many of them run their own businesses, because this is something which is encouraged by Sikh teaching, especially that of the fourth Guru, Guru Ram Das. It is also easier for Sikhs to practice their religion fully (for example by wearing the turban) if they are working for themselves.

For most people, Sikh men are easily recognizable by their turbans. Not all men who wear turbans are Sikhs (they may be Hindus or Muslims). And some Sikh men do not wear turbans, while some Sikh women do! People are not Sikhs because of what they wear, but because they follow the Gurus' teachings.

Above: Equality is a very important part of Sikh belief. Here men and women in a British Sikh community work together preparing the *langar*, the meal which Sikhs eat together to show that everyone is equal.

Left: Agriculture is a traditional Sikh occupation. These two men in the Punjab are plowing with oxen, just as their families have done for generations. This is an unusual sight in the Punjab, where most of the farming takes place now with the aid of machines.

How Sikhism began

The story of the Sikh religion begins with the ten great teachers known as the Gurus. The word "guru" means a holy man or teacher, and the word was used originally in the Hindu religion to describe those who taught groups of followers (or disciples). The first of the Sikh Gurus was Guru Nanak.

Guru Nanak

Guru Nanak was born in 1469 into a Hindu family. It is said that even as a child he seemed wiser than other children, and his teachers soon found they had nothing left to teach him. When he was ten it was time for him to take part in a Hindu ceremony for boys, when he would be given a special thread to wear around his shoulder for the rest of his life. Guru Nanak refused. He said that how people behaved and thought was more important than a thread which could wear out or get dirty.

As Guru Nanak grew older, his family thought that perhaps he would settle down and be more like other people if he got married, so when he was 19 a wife was found for him. Guru Nanak loved his wife, and was happy to be married, but it did not change the way he behaved. He went to join his sister's husband who worked in a town called Sultanpur. He began to sit each morning and evening singing hymns and meditating; gradually, more and more people came and joined him.

In the court of God

Early one morning, Guru Nanak went to the river to bathe. He disappeared; his friends searched everywhere but could not find him. Three days later, he returned, just as suddenly. The first thing he said was "There is neither Hindu nor Muslim;" he meant that going through the ceremonies of the Hindu or Muslim religions did not by itself make people closer to God. It was the way people lived and what they believed which counted most. Guru Nanak said that while he had been away, God had told him that he was to be a teacher and leader of people.

Gathering followers

Guru Nanak spent many years traveling around teaching, and visited Hindu and Muslim holy places, including the Muslim holy city of Mecca. Wherever he went, he taught that the way to God was not through ceremonies and rituals. When Guru Nanak was about 50 years old, he stopped traveling and set up a new town in the Punjab, which he called Kartarpur. It was there that a man whom Sikhs call *Bhai* Lehna came to see him and became the Guru's most trusted follower.

In 1539, Guru Nanak announced that Lehna was to be the next Guru. Guru Nanak had given Lehna a new name, Angad, which means "part of me." A few days later, Guru Nanak lay down quietly and died, but he had left Guru Angad to carry on his work.

Below: Sikh places of worship are sometimes decorated with scenes from the life of Guru Nanak. A Sikh artist painted this mural in a British gurdwara showing the Guru with his two sons and two of his followers.

Left: These Sikhs have traveled to the gurdwara in Nankana Sahib, the town where Guru Nanak was born. The town is named after Guru Nanak, and is now part of Pakistan. Sikhs from India are allowed to visit it in groups. These worshipers are seated to show their respect as the Guru Granth Sahib is being uncovered.

Left: Many stories are told about Guru Nanak. One tells of how he was invited to dinner by a poor man named Lalo. A rich officer called Malik Bhago also asked the Guru to dinner, and was annoyed because the Guru preferred to eat with Lalo.

The Guru showed Malik why. He accepted Malik's invitation to dinner, and went to his house. When he got there, he took some bread from each house and squeezed it. From Lalo's bread came milk, but from Malik Bhago's came blood. The Guru explained that Lalo, though poor, was honest, but Malik Bhago had made his money by exploiting other people.

The voice of God

Guru Nanak had two sons, and they were not pleased when he chose Guru Angad to carry on his work. They thought that one of them should be the next Guru, because Guru Nanak was their father. But Guru Nanak had chosen the person who was most ready and able to do the work. Guru Nanak had asked his sons several times to do tasks which seemed to them beneath their dignity. Each time they refused, and Guru Angad had obeyed instead, showing that he was the best person to become the next Guru.

All the Gurus who came after Guru Nanak were chosen in this way. It did not matter whether or not they were related to the Guru who came before them. The most important thing was that they were people who could carry on the work which Guru Nanak had begun. They had to have the abilities needed to teach and guide the Sikh people.

The written word

Nine Gurus followed Guru Nanak; some are remembered particularly for what they added to the Sikh faith. Guru Angad, the second Guru, helped to make it possible for Sikhs to read the hymns which Guru Nanak and the later Gurus composed. During his time, Punjabi, the language spoken by Sikhs, did not have a proper alphabet; there were a number of different ways in which people wrote Punjabi down. Guru Angad chose one particular way, and gave this alphabet a name – Gurmukhi. Today Sikhs learn to read Gurmukhi so that they can read the Sikh hymns, which are now always written in that alphabet.

Equality

When Guru Nanak was alive, he had encouraged everyone who visited him to sit down and eat together. This was most

Right: This crowd has gathered in Delhi for a festival in memory of Guru Tegh Bahadur, the ninth Guru. The banner shows the Guru being asked to choose between becoming a Muslim and being executed. His followers can be seen in the background.

unusual. Not all Hindus would eat together, and some Hindus would not eat with Muslims. The Guru wanted to show that in the sight of God everyone is equal. The third Guru, Guru Amar Das, carried on this tradition; he set up a *langar*, or open kitchen, where anyone could come and eat. Whoever wanted to see the Guru had to sit down and eat at the *langar* first.

The city of the Guru

The fourth Guru, Guru Ram Das, is best known for founding the Sikh holy city of Amritsar. The land where the city stands was given to the Sikhs by a Muslim emperor, Akbar, who had a great deal of respect for Guru Ram Das. The city began as a small town, at first named Ramdaspur after the Guru and then Amritsar, which means "pool of nectar." The town soon grew, and on festival days many Sikhs gathered there to celebrate together.

When Guru Arjan, who was the son of Guru Ram Das, became Guru (in 1581), he carried on his father's work at Amritsar by building a place of worship there for Sikhs. This temple was called *Harimandir*, which means "house of God," and later came to be known as the Golden Temple. It is still the major Sikh holy place. Guru Arjan also gathered together hymns which had been composed by the earlier Gurus. He added hymns of his own and some by Hindu and Muslim writers, and made these into a book which was called the Adi Granth (or first book). This book later came to be called the Guru Granth Sahib, the holy book of the Sikhs.

A time of struggle

Because the Sikh religion grew up in a part of India ruled by Muslims, it was sometimes not easy for people to be Sikhs. It began to be particularly difficult from the time of the sixth Guru, Guru Hargobind. He became Guru after his father, Guru Arjan, was tortured and drowned. Guru Hargobind was much more like a warrior than the earlier Gurus, and encouraged Sikhs to use swords and to ride horses. It was the start of a new way of life for Sikhs: they were beginning to be prepared to fight for their beliefs.

By the time of Guru Gobind Singh, the tenth Guru, the history of the Sikhs was one of persecution, torture and death. It was necessary to build the Sikhs into a fighting

force so that they could protect their faith; it was because of this that the Khalsa, the brotherhood of Sikhs, was begun by Guru Gobind Singh in the year 1699.

The last human leader

The ten Gurus led the Sikh community for well over two hundred years, from 1469 until 1708, when Guru Gobind Singh died. Unlike the Gurus who had come before him, Guru Gobind Singh did not choose another human being to become the next teacher of the Sikhs. He said that there were to be no more human Gurus. Instead, the book which contained the hymns of the Gurus was to be their teacher and guide from that time on. This book, which was made up of the Adi Granth and the hymns of the ninth Guru, Guru Tegh Bahadur, was known from that time as the Guru Granth Sahib, and it is still the teacher of the Sikhs.

Above: This Indian painting shows Guru Nanak and Guru Gobind Singh together, although they could never have met (Guru Nanak died over 100 years before Guru Gobind Singh was born).

The painting is a way of expressing the Sikh belief that the Gurus all shared the same spirit and teaching.

The Guru Granth Sahib

The Sikhs no longer had a human Guru to teach and guide them when Guru Gobind Singh died in 1708. He told them that they were to be guided instead by the words of the Gurus which had been written down and put into a book, the Guru Granth Sahib.

Many hymns of the Gurus as well as hymns written by people who were not Sikhs had already been gathered together by the time of Guru Amar Das. Guru Arjan, (the fifth Guru), then used these collections and other hymns (including his own), to put together the book known as the Adi Granth (or first book). This book was treated with great respect, and kept in the *Harimandir* at Amritsar. Guru Gobind Singh added his father's hymns to the Adi Granth, and then announced that the finished book was to be the next and last Sikh Guru.

Below: The Guru Granth Sahib is laid to rest in a special room of its own every night, and carried back to its place in the worship room each morning. It is always carried on the head of the person who brings it in. This is a way of showing how Sikhs always place the book above them because they hold it in such great respect.

Reading the book

The Guru Granth Sahib is written in the Gurmukhi script which Guru Angad developed, and all Sikhs need to learn to read Gurmukhi so that they can read the scriptures (another name for the book). It may be read out in the Sikh place of worship, the gurdwara, by any Sikh man or woman. Some gurdwaras have a person (known as a *granthi*) who is paid to be a full-time reader; he or she may also often act as a teacher. When it is being read the book is placed on a special platform and shaded by a canopy, or cloth hanging over it. A fan is waved over it, because the human Gurus had fans waved over them as a sign of respect.

Respect for the word

The Guru Granth Sahib is always treated by Sikhs with the same respect which they had for the human Gurus. No ceremony other than a funeral can take place unless it is there, and so it has an important place in every major event of a Sikh's life. It is not kept on a shelf with other books; when a family owns a copy, it has a special room to itself.

Any room where the Guru Granth Sahib is kept is treated as holy; it must be kept clean, and people entering must remove their shoes and cover their heads to show how they honor the book.

A personal guide

On special occasions, the Guru Granth Sahib is read right through from beginning to end. This is a lengthy task, since it contains 5,894 hymns and verses, and usually takes about forty-eight hours. Several people will take it in turns to read. In the past, copies of the Guru Granth Sahib were always handwritten, but towards the end of the 19th century they began to be printed. All copies of the Guru Granth Sahib are identical, and have 1,430 pages. Many Sikhs would like to have their own copy, but this is not always possible because they may not be able to read it, or give it a room of its own.

Guru Gobind Singh had told his followers that they were to be guided by the Guru Granth Sahib, and so Sikhs also use their holy book to provide them with advice. At the end of services the Guru Granth Sahib is opened at random, and several verses are read out, which will help those who hear them to live as Sikhs. Many Sikhs look for advice like this every day.

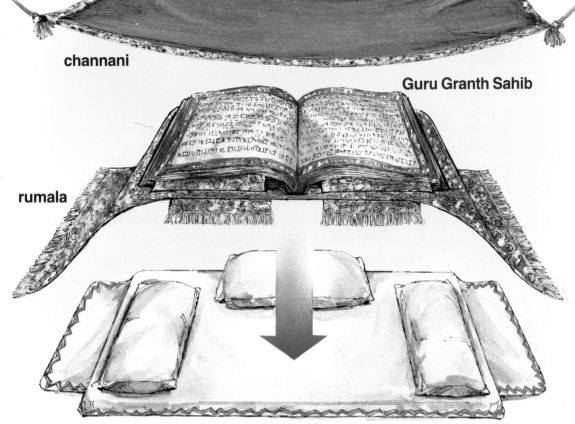

channani

Guru Granth Sahib

rumala

Manji Sahib

Left: The Guru Granth Sahib is treated with the same respect as the human Gurus received. The place where it rests is the most important and beautifully decorated part of the gurdwara.

The book is always carefully protected by a canopy hanging over it (called a *channani*), and by special cloths wrapped around it (known as the *rumala*). When the book is opened it rests on a quilt and three cushions, which together are called the *Manji Sahib*.

Left: Any Sikh man or woman may read in public from the Guru Granth Sahib, like this woman in Kenya. The pen which can be seen in the photograph has probably been used to write down a favorite passage in the book.

Basic beliefs

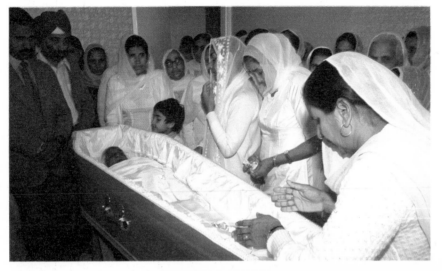

Sikhs believe that there is only one God, who created the universe and everything in it. They often call him *Sat Guru*, "true Guru," or *Waheguru*, "wonderful Guru." God is seen as being very different from anyone or anything that people know. For example, Sikhs believe that God has never had a human body, and so has never been born or ever died. Sikhs also believe that God is present everywhere.

Living in a body

For Sikhs, human life is only one of many possible kinds of life. The human bodies in which people live are not the only bodies they have ever had, or will ever have. Sikhs believe that they have lived before, perhaps as animals

Above: When Sikhs die, the family gathers to say goodbye to the person they have known. Afterwards, the body is not buried, but cremated. The cremation can take place on a funeral pyre (a large fire), or at a crematorium. The ashes are then scattered on running water (either a river or the sea).

Right: The Mool Mantra, the first hymn composed by Guru Nanak, sums up the basic beliefs of Sikhism. The symbol representing the first words, *Ik oankar* ('there is one God'), is found on the canopy above the Guru Granth Sahib. The top row of writing here is in Gurmukhi, the Punjabi script. The Mool Mantra is written at the beginning of every chapter in the Guru Granth Sahib.

ੴ
IK OANKAR
There is only one God

ਸਤਿ ਨਾਮੁ
SAT NAAM
Truth is his name

ਕਰਤਾ ਪੁਰਖ
KARTA PURKH
He is the creator

ਨਿਰ ਭਉ
NIR BHAU
He is without fear

ਨਿਰ ਵੈਰੁ
NIR VAIR
He is without hate

ਅਕਾਲ ਮੂਰਤਿ
AKAAL MOORAT
He is timeless and without form

ਅਜੂਨੀ ਸੈਭੰ
AJOONI SABHANG
He is beyond death, the enlightened one

ਗੁਰ ਪ੍ਰਸਾਦਿ ॥
GUR PARSAAD
He can be known by the Guru's grace

or plants, even as rocks and stones. But it is only when they are born into human bodies that they have the ability to respond to the love of the God who created them.

The world

Sikhs see human life as being good because God made it. Because it is good, people can care a lot about what life offers them. Sometimes people care too much; they become too attached to the pleasures of life, and love them rather than God. As long as people do this, Sikhs believe, they will go on being born into different bodies. And as long as they have a body, they cannot live totally with God.

Finding God

People can also rely too much on themselves. No one can find God just by his or her own efforts. God chooses to show himself to those whom he decides are ready. Sikhs try to make themselves ready by learning how to love God more than the world. The ten human Gurus were born to help people know how to live and love God. The teachings of the six Gurus written in the Guru Granth Sahib guide Sikhs in learning how to love God.

Human beings can begin to make themselves ready by prayer and by living the right sort of life, but even these on their own are not enough. Some people may spend many years praying, meditating and living a very good life without getting close to God, while others may do so very easily. When God has chosen someone to be close to him, Sikhs feel that God looks on the person in a special way. They call this *nadar* or "grace." Human beings may not understand why God shows grace to one person at a certain time, and not to another, but God knows when people are ready to be shown grace.

Death

Sikhs don't feel that they should mourn and be unhappy when someone dies. The main prayer used at Sikh funerals is the *Sohila Mahala* which Sikhs also say every night when they go to sleep. Sikhs feel there is no more reason to be sad when people die than there is when they go to sleep. Since a person lives many lives, death is just another stage in those lives.

To help the dead person's family realize that death is part of God's will, the Guru Granth Sahib is read from beginning to end after a

funeral. The funeral is also often followed by a feast, and gifts are made to charity.

The brotherhood

Most Sikhs share these beliefs about life, the world, death and God. Many Sikhs come to a point in their lives where they want to join the Khalsa, or brotherhood of Sikhs. Joining this brotherhood is a special way of saying what a Sikh believes.

Below: The example of Sikhs from earlier times helps to strengthen the beliefs of those living now. The armory at the Akal Takht at Amritsar contains the weapons of the *panj pyares*, the five beloved who were the first to join the Khalsa, or brotherhood of Sikhs.

The Khalsa

Some Sikhs join a special group which they call the Khalsa. They do this when they feel ready; some people wait until their children are grown up before they join.

The Khalsa ceremony does not have to take place in the gurdwara, but the holy book, the Guru Granth Sahib, and a reader (perhaps the *granthi*) must be present. Any five Sikhs who are already members of the Khalsa can carry out the ceremony. They fill an iron bowl with a drink called *amrit* and stir it with a sword. The candidates (those who want to join) drink

some, and what is left is sprinkled on their eyes and hair. The *granthi* tells the candidates that they are now children of Guru Gobind Singh and his wife Mata Sahib Kaur, and reminds them of how to live their lives as Khalsa Sikhs. At the end of the ceremony, everyone eats a little of the sweet food called *karah parshad*.

How the Khalsa began

In the 17th century the rulers of India were forcing people to become Muslims. In 1675 a group of Hindus asked Guru Tegh Bahadur, the ninth Sikh Guru, to help them save the Hindu religion. Guru Tegh Bahadur's son, Gobind Rai, told them only Guru Tegh Bahadur could help them.

Guru Tegh Bahadur went with several of the Sikhs to the Muslim court in the city of Delhi. They were all put in prison and told they would be killed if they would not become Muslims. They bravely chose to die rather than change their religious beliefs, and so were put to death.

The faithful ones

Guru Gobind Rai succeeded Tegh Bahadur as Guru. Twenty four years later Sikhs were still being persecuted, so he called all the Sikhs together during the April festival of Baisakhi. Then he asked if anyone among them was willing to die for the Sikh faith. Five men said they would. The Guru took each man away, and returned five times with a bloodstained sword. Everyone watching thought he had killed them.

Finally he went away and returned with all five men – alive! Guru Gobind Rai called them the *panj pyares* – the faithful ones. He made them members of the Khalsa, and gave them and himself the new name *Singh*, which means "lion," Then he told them they should wear special signs, known today as "the five K's," to show people that they were Sikhs. Many of the other Sikh men and women who had been watching came forward then and joined the Khalsa too. The women who joined were given the special name *Kaur*, which means "princess." Then everyone drank *amrit* together.

Left: At the Khalsa ceremony, five Sikhs represent the *panj pyares*, the first members of the Khalsa. They wear special clothes to show who they are; they may be men or women.

Special signs

When Guru Gobind Singh founded the Khalsa (or brotherhood of Sikhs), he said that all its members should wear five special signs to show that they were Sikhs. These signs are known as the five K's, because their names in Punjabi all begin with K. They are:

- *kesh* (uncut hair),
- *kanga* (comb),
- *kara* (steel wrist band),
- *kirpan* (sword)
- *kaccha* or *kacchera* (a kind of short trousers or underpants).

All Sikhs who have joined the Khalsa must wear the five K's; other Sikhs do not have to, but many choose to wear some or all of them. Guru Gobind Singh did not just choose the signs without thinking. Each sign has a meaning, and wearing even one of them helps Sikhs to remember what the Sikh religion and the teachings of the Gurus are all about.

Below: The five K's are: top left, *kanga*; middle left, *kesh*; bottom left, *kaccha*; top right, *kirpan*; and bottom right, *kara*.

All for a reason

Holy men in India often did not cut their hair, but some let it become tangled and dirty. Sikhs must keep the *kesh* clean and tidy, and so their hair must be combed at least twice a day. The *kanga* or comb with which this is done reminds Sikhs that their lives should also be tidy and well-ordered.

The *kara* or steel bracelet is a circle, so it reminds Sikhs that God is one, without a beginning or an end. It also reminds them that the Khalsa is one, joined together in unity. The material which the *kara* is made of is important; it is not made of a soft metal like gold or silver. Instead it is made of steel, which is hard and strong, showing that Sikhs must be strong when they are fighting for what is right.

The *kirpan* or sword also reminds Sikhs that they are warriors. Sikhs must always remember that they are warriors. But they must also

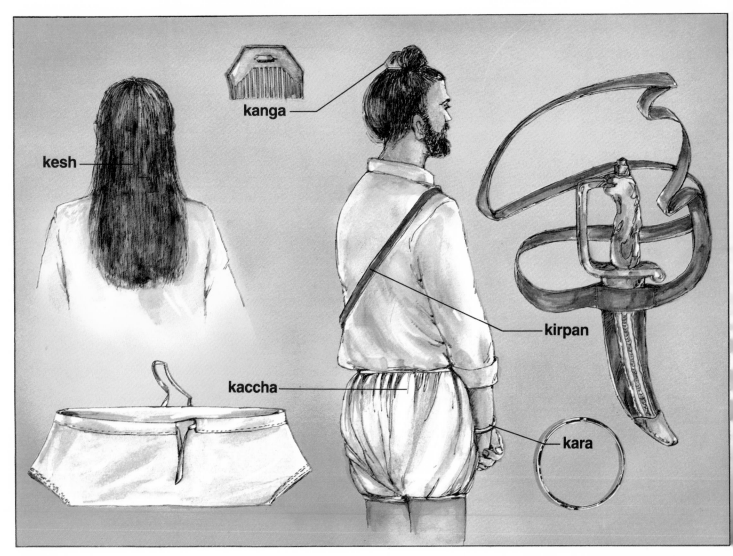

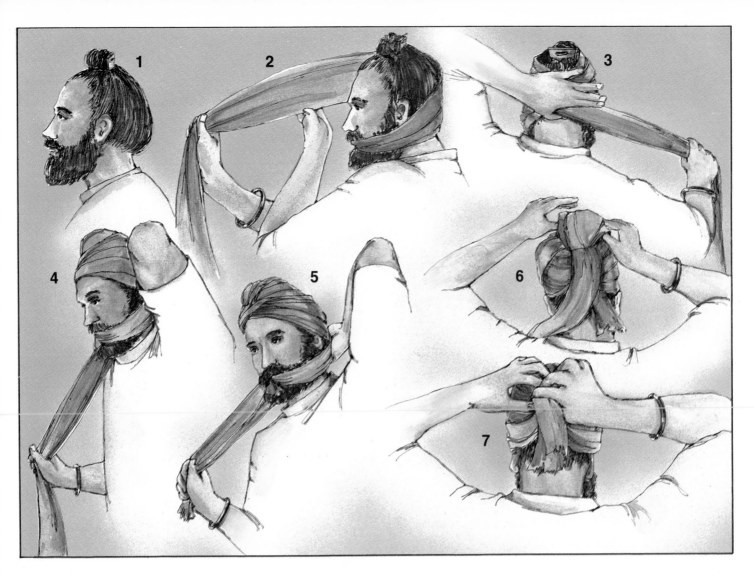

remember that the *kirpan* is not a weapon for attacking people, but for defending Sikh beliefs and protecting the weak and helpless.

In Guru Gobind Singh's time, most Indians dressed in a dhoti, which was a long piece of cloth wrapped and tied around them. It was difficult to fight dressed in a dhoti, and so the Guru told the Khalsa that they were to wear *kaccha*, which would allow them to move more easily. Sikhs outside India often wear the *kaccha* underneath Western clothes.

The turban

The turban is not one of the signs which the Guru told the Khalsa to wear, but most male Sikhs wear turbans. Guru Gobind Singh told Sikhs that they should try to be as much like him as possible. Sikhs do this by living their lives as much like the Guru as they can, but they also try to look as the Guru did in his lifetime. In India the turban was a sign of authority worn by rulers and powerful men. Guru Gobind Singh wore a turban to show that Sikhs were powerful, and so Sikhs wear turbans to be like the Guru.

Turbans can be worn in many different colors, though some groups of Sikhs choose to wear a particular color of turban. Each turban is a long piece of cloth, and it is tied every day; boys usually begin wearing a turban as soon as they can tie it for themselves. Lengths of material for turbans are often given as gifts on special occasions.

Special problems

Sikhs outside India sometimes find that there are problems when they wear the turban and the five K's. In some jobs, for example ones where workers wear uniforms with special hats, it is not always easy for Sikhs to be allowed to wear their turbans. A law was introduced in Britain which said that everyone had to wear a crash helmet when riding a motorcycle. Sikhs objected to this because a crash helmet will not fit over a turban. Eventually they were told they did not have to wear crash helmets. The *kirpan* has caused problems too; although it is a weapon which should only be used for protecting what is right, people who do not understand its purpose often think of it only as a dangerous weapon. To get over this problem, many Sikhs wear a small imitation *kirpan* set into the *kanga*, or comb.

Above: Tying a turban is a difficult task to learn, but Sikhs become expert at it in time! This is one way, but different people have their own particular ways: **1** The hair is fixed in place with the *kanga*. **2** The cloth is wound round the head, keeping one end in the teeth. **3** The back of the head is pressed with one hand and the cloth pulled tight with the other. **4** The winding still continues. **5** Almost finished; only a short bit left. **6** The short bit is tucked into the top of the turban, and spread to cover the hair. **7** Now the end that's been in the teeth is tucked in to finish the turban completely.

Being a Sikh

Right: Although the basic beliefs by which Sikhs live their lives have stayed the same since the time of Guru Nanak, the ways in which they work have changed. These are Sikh truck drivers parked beside a road in a part of northern India.

22

The way people live their lives as Sikhs can vary from person to person, but there are certain guidelines which should be followed. Some of these are religious requirements for Sikhs, while others are seen as rules by which all human beings, not just Sikhs, should live.

All Sikhs should study their scriptures, first by learning to read (and write) the Gurmukhi script in which they are written, and then by studying the lives and teachings of the Gurus. In this way they can learn to understand the difference between God and the Gurus whom he created; they can also learn the right and wrong way to live their lives from the Gurus' teachings. Sikhs should spend time meditating about God, as well as reading and studying the scriptures. This means that they should make time to sit and think quietly about God.

Left: Sikhs do not only practice their religion in the gurdwara; it is just as important to think quietly about God at home.

Food

There are certain things which all Sikhs should avoid doing (Khalsa members promise not to do them). All Sikhs try to observe the rule that they should not eat meat prepared in certain ways, because the tenth Guru said that those ways were cruel to animals. Sikhs cannot eat meat killed according to Muslim or Jewish religious practices. And, because Sikhism began and grew up in a country where there were many Hindus, many Sikhs will not eat beef, out of respect for the belief of Hindus around them (although Sikhs do not believe the cow is sacred). Just as some people from other religions choose to be vegetarians, some Sikhs choose not to eat meat at all, but this is a personal choice, not a rule.

Mind and body

Sikhs should also avoid the use of tobacco and alcohol, and not use any other drugs except for medical reasons. In the Guru Granth Sahib, several of the Gurus, including Guru Nanak, point out the bad effects of these substances. Guru Gobind Singh also gave many practical examples of how they affect mind and body.

Guru Gobind Singh intended Khalsa members to live their lives as warriors, and so he warned them not to use tobacco, alcohol or drugs, because using these things would slow them down physically and mentally. This would give the enemy an advantage and put the lives of other Khalsa members in danger. It would also make them more vulnerable to disease and illness.

Attitudes to others

Sikhs should not gamble or steal, and they should be loyal to their husbands and wives. To help them keep these rules, Sikhs should pray every day; they should also visit the gurdwara as often as possible, so that they can study and pray with other Sikhs.

Service to the community is also very important for Sikhs. They should be prepared to give their time and energy (and sometimes money) to those around them. Sikhs feel they should give in this way to everyone.

Above: The family is very important for Sikhs. All the members of this Canadian Sikh family work together at their fruit farm, picking blueberries.

The gurdwara

Above: The symbol of Sikhism which is seen on the flag outside all gurdwaras is made up of three parts. On the outside are two swords. These show that Sikhs should serve God by teaching the truth, and by fighting to defend what is right. The circle is a reminder to all Sikhs that God is one. In the middle is the *khanda*, the double-edged sword used to prepare *amrit*.

Right: This is a traditional *langar*, where everyone sits on the floor, but at many gurdwaras people sit on benches at tables. Food is often served in steel trays which have a section for each sort of food. The people serving the food have scarves around their mouths to stop any saliva from accidentally getting onto the food.

When Sikhs gather together for worship, they usually do so in a special building known as a gurdwara, which means "door of the Guru" or "God's house." Services can be held anywhere as long as the Guru Granth Sahib is present, but most take place in the gurdwara.

Different shapes, one purpose
The gurdwara is at the heart of the Sikh community, but it is not the building itself which is so important; it is the gathering together of Sikhs in the presence of the Guru Granth Sahib which gives the gurdwara its special place in Sikh life.

Gurdwaras can come in many different shapes or sizes: some are specially built, while others, especially outside India, are houses or other buildings which have been converted for the purpose. All gurdwaras, however, have certain features in common. No one is allowed to bring tobacco, alcohol or any other intoxicating drug into the gurdwara. Gurdwaras also always have a special room where services are held, and another where the Guru Granth Sahib is kept when it is not in the worship room.

The worship room
Outside this room there is a place to leave shoes, because everyone who goes into it must first take off their shoes and cover their head as a sign of respect (usually someone looks after the shoes!). As people enter they place offerings of food and money on the carpet in front of the special platform on which the Guru Granth Sahib rests. After people have made their offering they bow to the scriptures, and then sit down.

Days for worship
Sikhs do not have a special day for worship, so the main service of the week takes place on the rest day of the particular country the gurdwara is in: for example, in Muslim countries, it takes place on a Friday, while in other countries such as Britain, Canada and the United States the main service is on a Sunday.

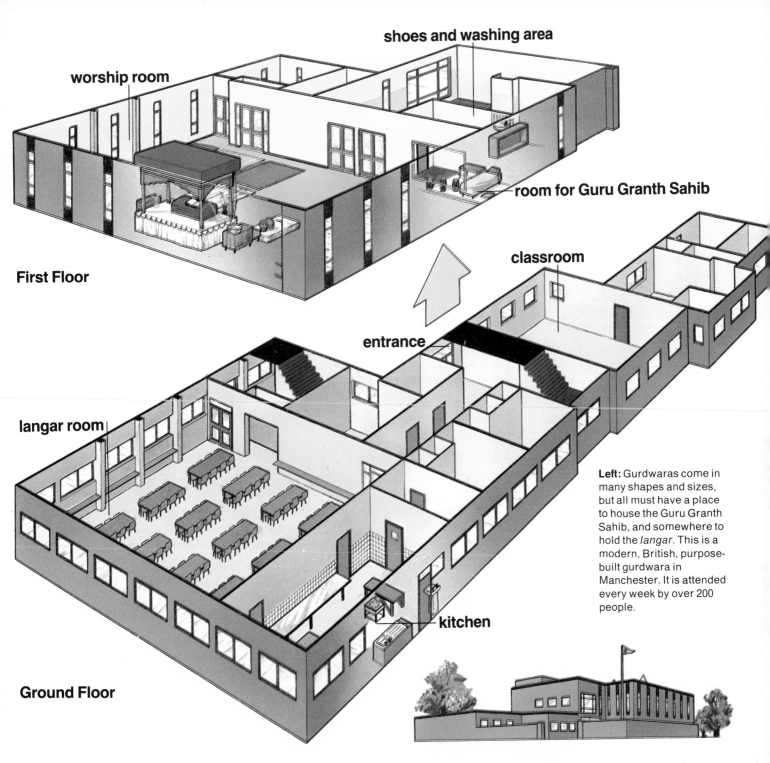

worship room

shoes and washing area

room for Guru Granth Sahib

First Floor

classroom

entrance

langar room

Left: Gurdwaras come in many shapes and sizes, but all must have a place to house the Guru Granth Sahib, and somewhere to hold the *langar*. This is a modern, British, purpose-built gurdwara in Manchester. It is attended every week by over 200 people.

kitchen

Ground Floor

A typical service

During the service, people come in, sit on the floor (which is carpeted), and leave when they want to. Men and women sit separately; this is just custom and there is no religious reason for it. Most of the service involves the singing of hymns from the Guru Granth Sahib.

At the end of the service, certain special hymns will be sung, which everyone joins in, and all the congregation stands up to say a prayer called *Ardas*. The *granthi* then opens the Guru Granth Sahib at random and reads a few verses, which will help to give the congregation guidance for that day. While *Ardas* is being said, a bowl containing a candy made of flour, water, sugar and butter is stirred with a short sword (a *kirpan*), and at the end of the service everyone is given some of this candy, known as *karah parshad*.

A community center

Services are only one of the many activities that take place in the gurdwara. The gurdwara is not just a place of worship; it is also a meeting place which tries to serve the needs of the community. For Sikhs, one of the most important of these needs is to teach Gurmukhi. Every Sikh needs to be able to read the Guru Granth Sahib, and so children attend classes at the gurdwara.

Above: The Sikh flag is always flown outside a gurdwara. Often the flagpole is on top of the building; here it is on ground level, but the flag itself is always higher than the building.

Songs to God

Prayer is an important part of most religions, and Sikhism is no exception to this. Sikhs who are members of the Khalsa make a promise to say certain prayers every day, but all Sikhs will try to make at least some time during the day to pray and to think about God.

Praying at home

Outside India, Sikhs do not always have much time to pray and so they may have to do it while they are busy with other activities in the morning. Busy housewives may pray while preparing breakfast; workers sometimes pray while driving to work, and some even have tapes of prayers which they play on the car stereo and join in with. The length of the prayer can also vary. Some Sikhs recite the whole 38 verses of the morning prayer (or *Japji Sahib*), either by heart or by reading from the *gutkha*, a book containing hymns from the Guru Granth Sahib. Others who have less time may recite the first five verses. Those who have very little time, or cannot read the verses and do not know them by heart, may just repeat the name of God, *Waheguru*, which means "wonderful Lord."

The *Japji Sahib* is a prayer which tells how everything is made by God and under God's control. So all Sikhs start their day by remembering that there is only one God, who is all-powerful and should be worshiped. The first words of the prayer are "In the beginning there was truth."

In the evening, at the end of a day's work, Sikhs often recite the *Rahiras*, or listen to it being recited. This prayer thanks God for the successes of the day. When people do well in life it is very easy for them to feel that they have done it all by themselves, and so they may become conceited and selfish. Sikhs remind themselves that everything which they have comes from God, and should be given back to God. God is addressed as "You the Giver, You the Receiver."

Praying at the gurdwara

As well as praying at home, a Sikh can join in prayer with others at the gurdwara. Although they can do this on any day, most Sikhs visit the gurdwara on the usual day of rest of the country in which they live. This means that the whole family can go to the gurdwara.

Right: Like this old man, Sikhs in India usually have more time to pray than Sikhs in other countries. They often rise before dawn for the morning prayer. As well as reading hymns from the *gutkha*, Sikhs often use beads in their prayer at home. They recite the name of God a number of times, counting off his name on the beads as they recite.

Quite often, the opening hymn, *Asa da Vaar*, will be sung by the *granthi* alone. Since not all Sikhs know this prayer well enough to sing it, some gurdwaras which do not have a full-time *granthi* or anyone else who can sing the *Asa da Vaar* will play a tape recording of it for the congregation.

Ardas

Towards the end of the service, the congregation sings the *Anand Sahib*, a hymn composed by Guru Amar Das which is about the joy of finding God. This is followed by *Ardas*, the one prayer for which every member of the congregation stands; they stay seated for the other prayers. *Ardas* asks Sikhs to remember God and the Gurus, and to think of those who have died for the Sikh faith. It asks God to keep Sikhs faithful and to bless the whole world. Special prayers can be added to suit the occasion (for example, at a wedding). At the end of *Ardas*, the words "*Waheguru ji khalsa, Waheguru ji ki fateh*" are said. This means "The Khalsa belongs to God, victory belongs to God." The same prayers are used even on special occasions such as weddings.

Left: This Sikh woman is singing *Kirtan Sohila*, the last prayer of the day, at home. The woman is one of the growing number of non-Indian Canadian Sikhs. The prayer they are saying reminds them that life is short, so they must spend their time well. One line tells them: "Days and nights are running out of your life," and so they must use the time they have in serving God.

Below: The singing of hymns (known as *Kirtan*) is an important part of Sikh services. These young Sikhs are being taught to play the hymns at a gurdwara school.

Service to others

Service to others is a very important part of the Sikh religion. Ever since the time of the Gurus, Sikhs have shown their faith by their service to other people; the Sikh name for this service is *sewa*.

When people think about helping others, they often think about giving money. Guru Gobind Singh said that Sikhs should try to give a tenth of their income, but no one is forced to do this. Some people cannot afford to give so much. Sikhs often bring food to help make the *kara parshad* which is shared after every service. Sikh shopkeepers may give food without payment if it is for the gurdwara, or if they cannot afford to give the food they may charge less than the normal price.

Giving time and effort

Giving money is not the most important way for Sikhs to serve others. *Sewa* can mean giving time and energy to help other people. Often the jobs involved are ones which might be looked down on. The Gurus themselves were often chosen because of their willingness to serve others in whatever way was needed.

Guru Nanak chose his successor, *Bhai* Lehna, (who became Guru Angad) in this way. One night it was raining heavily, and part of Guru Nanak's house fell down. The Guru asked his two sons to rebuild it, but they refused. They said it was too late and too cold.

Bhai Lehna got up at once and began to rebuild the wall. Each time he rebuilt it, the Guru said it was built wrong, and *Bhai* Lehna took the wall down and began to build it again.

The Guru was pleased with his patience and willingness to work. *Bhai* Lehna did tasks like this for the Guru several times before Guru Nanak eventually decided he was the right person to be the next Guru.

Help for all

Service to others does not just include service to Sikhs. On one occasion when the Sikhs were fighting a battle, some Sikhs came to Guru Gobind Singh with a complaint. They said that a water-carrier named Ghanaya was giving water to the enemy.

Guru Gobind Singh called in the water-carrier and asked if this was true. Ghanaya said that he had not helped any enemy. As he went around the battlefield, he did not see Sikhs or non-Sikhs; he saw the Guru in every man. When Guru Gobind Singh heard this, he gave Ghanaya ointment to put on the wounds of the soldiers he helped. He said that Ghanaya was to have the title of *Bhai* from then on, to show that the Guru honored him.

Some Sikhs can give a great deal of their time to help others, though even those who have very little time will try to find some act of *sewa* that they can do. Those who have more time may help with day-care centers for elderly people, or help out at a hospital, or do translation work.

Below: These Sikhs are giving their time and energy to help with the construction of a new gurdwara in Canada. Men, women and children all work together.

Talking about God

A third way of performing *sewa* is to talk to people about God. Sikhs do not try to convert other people to Sikhism. They encourage people to think about what their own religion says, and to live by its ideas. Guru Nanak himself went to Muslim and Hindu holy places, talking to people. He did not tell them that they should stop being Hindus or Muslims. Instead, he told them that they should be Hindus and Muslims because of what they believed, not because they carried out certain actions and rituals. Guru Nanak said that people should believe in and love God; then it did not matter if they were Hindus or Muslims. This is perhaps the most important form of *sewa*; giving people money or physical help only lasts for a short time, but giving people a new way of looking at their beliefs can last throughout their lives.

Above: Giving water to pilgrims who come to visit Sikh holy places, especially Amritsar, is a popular way to perform *sewa*. A drink of water is very welcome to a weary traveler in a hot country.

Left: Sikhs often perform *sewa* by helping to clean the gurdwara, or by looking after people's shoes while the owners are taking part in the service inside the gurdwara.

Marriage

Sikhs see marriage as being very important: all the Gurus were married apart from the boy Guru Har Krishan, and Guru Nanak said that people should not stay single. Marriage is particularly important for Sikhs because it is the basis for bringing up children in the Sikh faith. Marriage involves not just the couple getting married but also their families, and because of this the choice of marriage partner is made with the advice and assistance of the families. The couple usually meets before the wedding, but there will always be other people present. The most important thing about the choice of partners is that the bride and groom should both be Sikhs; a Sikh should not marry someone who is not also a Sikh.

Giving presents

Before the wedding ceremony itself, there is often an engagement ceremony; this does not have to take place, but if it does the Guru Granth Sahib should be present. During this ceremony the men from both families gather together and give each other gifts. The bridegroom is given gifts of sweet foods and money. The bride and her female relatives

have their own ceremony, where the bride has her hands painted with a red dye. Like her husband-to-be, she is given sweet foods and money. The groom's relatives send the bride jewelry and a red chunni (head scarf), and she wears these at the engagement ceremony.

Two become one

The wedding does not have to take place at the gurdwara, but in many areas it is usually held there. Wherever the ceremony takes place, the Guru Granth Sahib must be present. The bride wears either red trousers (shalwar) and tunic (kameez), or a red sari (which is one single piece of cloth), as well as a red headscarf and gold jewelry. Besides his turban, the groom may wear Indian or Western dress.

As long as both families agree, any Sikh may be in charge of the ceremony. Because it is such an important state for Sikhs, the ceremony begins with an explanation of what marriage is all about. The couple shows that they agree to be married by bowing towards the Guru Granth Sahib. Then the bride's father ties the bride's scarf (or chunni) to the scarf which the groom wears, showing that now she has left her father's care to join her husband's family.

The fourth Guru, Guru Ram Das, wrote a hymn which has four verses, each explaining something about marriage. This hymn is sung at Sikh weddings and, after each verse, the couple walks together around the Guru Granth Sahib. Their relatives help them around to show their support for the couple. When they have walked around four times, the closing hymns are sung and final prayers are read from the Guru Granth Sahib. Then everyone shares the sweet food *karah parshad*.

After the wedding

The women of the bride's family lead the groom away after the service and tease him before he can join everyone in a meal. The couple then visits the bride's home before they set out for the groom's family.

If one of the couple dies, the other is free to marry again. If the marriage breaks up, both families make great efforts to try to solve the problems. If this is not possible, Sikhs can divorce each other; there is no special ceremony or requirement, so a civil divorce is recognized. Divorced Sikhs may marry again in the gurdwara.

Below: Sikh brides-to-be often take part in a traditional ceremony before the wedding. This young woman's hands and feet are being decorated with patterns drawn in henna (a red dye). Such decoration is a social custom, not a religious requirement.

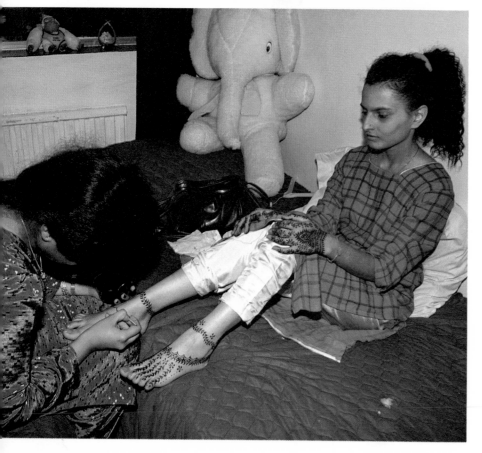

Left: Some Sikh weddings, like this one, are very traditional in style. The way the couple dresses and other details are a matter of custom, not belief. But walking around the Guru Granth Sahib (as this couple is doing) is always part of the ceremony.

Below: When a couple marries their families usually receive gifts. Sometimes it's the couple themselves who receive the gifts (as in this photograph).

Bringing up children

It is very important to Sikhs for their children to be brought up in a way which helps them to learn about the Sikh beliefs and way of life. When the family lives outside India, Sikhs believe it is especially important for children to be encouraged to keep their culture and traditions. The gurdwara can do a great deal to help the children to learn about their religion. If grandparents, aunts and uncles live with or near the children they can help to teach them, but parents have to take most of the responsibility for bringing their children up to know and understand Sikhism.

Choosing a name

Shortly after a new baby is born to a Sikh family, it makes its first visit to the gurdwara. This visit usually takes place as soon as the baby comes home from the hospital (if it was born in one) and has a special purpose – to give the new baby a first name. All the near relatives are contacted, and meet together at the gurdwara.

The ceremony takes place as part of the usual weekly service at the gurdwara. The service usually begins before the family arrives, since it is difficult to arrive early and stay

through a long service with a newborn baby. The group of musicians will choose hymns to sing which show how grateful the parents are to God for their new son or daughter. During the *Ardas* (or prayer said by everyone) it is usual to mention the name of the child's parents, and to thank God for giving them the strength and faith to bring their newborn child with them to the gurdwara.

Princesses and lions

After the *Ardas*, a random message from the Guru Granth Sahib is read out. It is from this reading that the name of the child is chosen. The *granthi* announces which letter of the alphabet the reading begins with, and the family then chooses a first name which begins with this letter.

Sikhs often do not have different first names for boys and girls, but it is easy to tell if a particular name belongs to a boy or a girl. Boys have the last name *Singh*, which means "lion," and girls have the last name *Kaur*, which means "princess." Sikhs all share these last names to show that they belong to one big family, the family of Sikhs.

After the child has been given a first name, the *granthi* gives it *amrit*, the mixture of sugar and water stirred with a sword which is also given to Sikhs when they join the Khalsa.

The growing child

At the naming ceremony, the *granthi* usually gives the child its first *kara* or steel bracelet, one of the five K's. Very small *karas* are made for tiny babies. As the child gets older, the *kara* will become too small, so it will be exchanged for a larger one. As the smaller *kara* is removed, a larger one is immediately placed on the child's wrist, since Sikhs should wear the *kara* at all times.

As the child grows up, he or she will have birthdays, but they will not usually have birthday parties for children their own age. Sikh birthday parties are normally family affairs, where all the child's family gets together to celebrate the birthday. Sometimes the family will pay for a *langar* at the gurdwara in honor of the child's birthday. Sikhs do not usually give presents at birthdays; instead, they may give the parents money to buy things for the child. Some Sikh families outside India are changing how they celebrate birthdays, but many still keep to the traditional ways.

Below: Sikh children wear their long hair in several different styles. Girls may put their hair in braids (like the girl here). or wear the scarf known as a chunni. When boys are young, they cover their hair with a piece of cloth called a *patkha*, but they are given a turban as soon as they are old enough to tie it (this is often when they are about five years old). A boy may be taught to tie his turban by his father, but quite often his mother teaches him, even though she has never worn a turban.

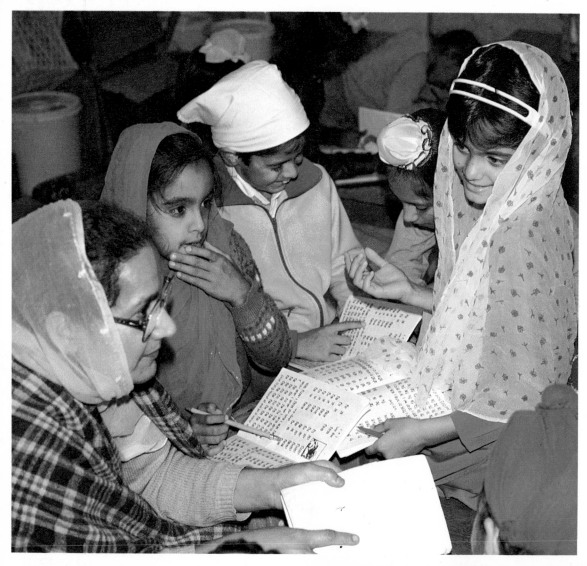

Left: Many Sikh children outside India cannot read very much Gurmukhi. As in other countries, these Canadian children go to special classes at the gurdwara, so that they can learn to read the Guru Granth Sahib and understand the services at the gurdwara.

Below: Children are encouraged to take part in religious activities. This girl is giving a talk about her religion at the festival of Baisakhi.

Learning and living

When the child is old enough, he or she can begin to learn about the Sikh religion. A Sikh child can learn in many different ways. Since the mother will often recite her prayers as she goes about her household tasks, the child may begin to learn them from her. Parents, grandparents and other relatives may tell the children stories about the Gurus when they are very young, and so they will gradually learn about the message of the Gurus.

The gurdwara also has classes for children where they can learn about their religion. In India some children may be able to read from the Guru Granth Sahib at 11 or 12 years of age, but the Sikh holy book is difficult to read, and British or American Sikh children who have to learn Gurmukhi first may be adults before they can read from the Guru Granth Sahib.

While Sikh children are learning about their religion, they are also carrying it out in practice. They are expected to wear the five K's, and in particular they will keep the *kesh* or uncut hair. They will often have to wash and dry their hair almost every day.

Holy places

There are four places which are particularly important for Sikhs because they are the places where decisions are made about the Sikh faith. These are: the Sri Akal Takht Sahib at Amritsar; the Takht Sri Patna Sahib at Patna; the Takht Sri Keshgarh Sahib at Anandpur; and the Takht Sri Hazur at Nander. The word "*takht*" means throne, and is often used to describe the platform where the Guru Granth Sahib rests in a gurdwara's worship room. The four *takhts* in India are special because Sikhs see them as places of authority.

Amritsar

The best known and most important holy place for Sikhs is Amritsar, which was founded by the fourth Guru, Guru Ram Das. The Guru had a pool built there when the land was given to the Sikhs, and a city grew up around it. Guru Arjan, the fifth Guru, had a temple built in the middle of the pool. The design of the temple was different from that of Hindu temples, where people climb steps up to the worship room. In this temple, four entrances were made to show that all who wished to enter could do so, and from which people descend into the worship room as a sign of humility.

Marble, jewels and gold

At the beginning of the 19th century Maharaja Ranjit Singh decided to have the temple at

Above: Many weapons belonging to the Gurus and their followers are housed in the armory shown here at Anandpur.

Right: Pilgrims who have come to visit the Golden Temple at Amritsar bathing in the pool before entering the Temple itself.

Amritsar rebuilt in marble. It was inlaid with semi-precious stones and covered with gold leaf, so it became known from then on as the Golden Temple. The golden walls have verses from the Guru Granth Sahib written on them.

Many pilgrims visit Amritsar, and before entering the Golden Temple they bathe first in the pool around it. One reason why so many pilgrims go there is because it contains some of the first copies ever made of the Guru Granth Sahib. When Guru Arjan gathered together the Adi Granth, he placed it in the temple at Amritsar.

The Guru Granth Sahib is continuously read through from beginning to end all day at the Golden Temple. It is kept in a special treasury over the gateway, and brought in each morning in a casket carried on the shoulders of several Sikhs.

Takht Sri Patna Sahib

Patna Sahib, which is 500 miles east of Delhi, is the birthplace of Guru Gobind Singh. The Guru spent his early childhood there, and many stories are told about his boyhood.

One tells about a Rani (or queen) named Mania. She had no children, and was very sad about this. She saw the Guru, who was a little boy about four years old at the time, and wished she could have a child like him. The Guru realized why she was so unhappy, and told her that she could treat him as her son.

Mania often gave him maize (a type of corn) to eat, and so maize is served at the *langar* in Patna Sahib. There is an armory at Patna Sahib, where weapons of the Guru are displayed on special occasions.

Anandpur

Anandpur is another very important place for Sikhs. It lies in a valley at the foot of the Himalayas. The ashes of the ninth Guru's head (Guru Tegh Bahadur) were buried there after he was killed. It was also at Anandpur that Guru Gobind Singh gathered his Sikhs together at Baisakhi and formed the Khalsa.

Takht Sri Hazur

Guru Gobind Singh is also associated with another Sikh holy place, the temple of Hazur Sahib in Nander (a town in southern India). This temple was built by Maharajah Ranjit Singh at the place where Guru Gobind Singh

died. In the treasury of the temple there are many of the Guru's possessions, including weapons, jewelry and clothing. Even a horse which is a descendant of the one the Guru used during his lifetime is kept in the stable, and led out in a procession on special occasions.

Pilgrims visit the holy places at all times of the year, but at the times of Sikh festivals they are particularly crowded with visitors from all parts of the world.

Above: The weaponry shown here is housed in the Hazur Sahib in Nander, the town where Guru Gobind Singh died. The Sikh nearby is wearing a set of prayer beads around his neck.

Times for celebration

Below: These two Sikh girls are celebrating Diwali at home in Britain. The festival has special meaning for Sikhs, but they also follow the Hindu custom of lighting candles at this time.

Sikhs have two main kinds of festival: those which are held on the same day as Hindu festivals but which have a special meaning for Sikhs, and those which celebrate events in the lives of the Gurus. Three major Sikh festivals are held on the same day as Hindu festivals: Baisakhi; Diwali; and Holi (which has become the Sikh Hola Mohalla). Guru Amar Das said that Sikhs should gather together for worship during Baisakhi and Diwali. This meant that people had to make up their minds whether they were Sikhs or Hindus, because they had to choose which gathering to attend. Guru Gobind Singh added Holi as another of the times when Sikhs should gather together.

Gathering the harvest

Baisakhi is celebrated in April, at the time of the harvest in India, and Sikhs used to gather together to give thanks to God and to listen to the teachings of the Guru. Guru Gobind Singh gave the festival a new meaning in 1699, because it was when the Sikhs were all gathered together for that year's Baisakhi that he founded the Khalsa. In memory of this, Sikhs who want to join the Khalsa often do so at Baisakhi.

Sikhs all over the world celebrate Baisakhi, but it is a particularly important occasion at Amritsar: many pilgrims come to the Golden Temple, and political rallies take place. Many events in Sikh history have happened at Baisakhi because Sikhs gather together in such numbers at this festival. One of the saddest festivals was in 1919. The British who ruled India at that time had forbidden the Sikhs to gather for Baisakhi, because they were afraid the Sikhs would rise up against them. Nevertheless, Sikhs did gather together for their festival, in a place called Jallianwala Bagh, in Amritsar. The army fired on them, and hundreds of Sikhs died that day.

Right: Each year, on the third day of the festival of Baisakhi, the gurdwara flag is taken down, changed and washed.

36

To freedom with the Guru

Diwali, which is held in either October or November, is the Hindu festival of light, but for Sikhs it is a particular reminder of the imprisonment and release of Guru Hargobind.

The sixth Guru had been imprisoned by the Emperor Jehangir along with fifty-two Hindu princes in the fort of Gwalior. At Diwali, the Emperor decided to release Guru Hargobind, but the Guru said that he would not leave prison unless the Hindu princes were also set free. The Emperor said that only those who could pass through a narrow passage holding onto the Guru's clothes would be released. It seemed impossible: how could the Guru get through the passage with fifty-two people holding onto him all at the same time? The Guru found a way around this. He had a cloak brought to him which had long tassels on the ends of it, and by holding onto these every one of the princes walked out to freedom with the Guru. At Diwali the Golden Temple is lit up, there are fireworks displays and people give candies to their relatives and friends. The day is also celebrated by services in the gurdwara.

Fairs and holidays

Holi is a festival where Hindus make merry and splash each other with colored water. Guru Gobind Singh decided that Sikhs ought to spend this time differently, and so Hola Mohalla, the three-day Sikh festival held at this time, became a time for Sikhs to train as soldiers. There were mock battles, and contests in horsemanship and wrestling.

This festival is still celebrated at Anandpur with a fair where many events take place, including singing, discussions, and competitions of physical skill.

Sikhs also celebrate festivals called *gurpurbs*, or holidays of the Gurus. Some of them are local festivals, but three are celebrated worldwide. These are the birthday of Guru Nanak in November; the birthday of Guru Gobind Singh in December or January; and the day on which Guru Arjan was martyred, which falls in May or June. During a *gurpurb*, the Guru Granth Sahib is often read right through from beginning to end. During the local festivals in India the holy book is often carried in a procession through the streets.

Above: These dancers are called Bhangra dancers, and often perform at Sikh festivals. Although the dance is not religious, performances like this one have been part of life in the Punjab for generations.

Sikhs in the Punjab

After the death of Guru Gobind Singh in 1708, the Sikhs managed to maintain the organization which the Guru had built up. They had been banded together into a military force, and were determined to create a land for themselves where they were free to practice their religion and not be persecuted for their beliefs. One of Guru Gobind Singh's companions, Banda Singh, gathered together a band of Sikhs and captured the town of Sirhind in 1710.

Although this helped Sikhs to gain control of the Punjab, it also led to further persecution. An order was given in that year for all Sikhs to be killed. For over half a century the Sikhs were mainly bands of wandering warriors, living in the hills and wildernesses, because they were in danger of death if they settled anywhere else.

By the middle of the 18th century, the rulers of northern India had been defeated by the armies of the King of Afghanistan. Now that they did not have to fight their former rulers, the Sikhs gathered together into twelve military groups and drove the invaders from Afghanistan out of the Punjab.

Maharajah Ranjit Singh

With that done, the Sikhs controlled the Punjab, but they had to decide among themselves who should be overall ruler. There was some disagreement, but eventually a young man proved himself to be a suitable leader by capturing the capital city of Lahore. This man, Ranjit Singh, was 19 years old when he captured Lahore; by the time he was 20, he became the ruler of the Punjab, with the title of Maharajah.

Maharajah Ranjit Singh was a strong but fair ruler. Although he himself was a Sikh,

Right: The area of India where Sikhism began is known as the Punjab; the name means "five rivers." The Punjab is not a separate country, but it is regarded as a special area by Sikhs, who ruled the Punjab for many years from Lahore, which was their capital city. Nankana Sahib, where Guru Nanak was born, is nearby.

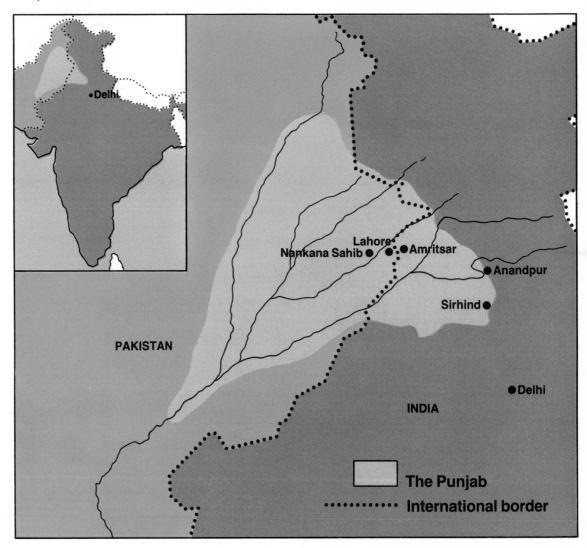

Left: These Sikhs are taking part in the rice harvest in the Punjab. Their van has prayers in Gurmukhi written all around its sides.

many of his officials were Muslims or Hindus; he did not discriminate against people because of their religion. During his reign, which lasted forty years, the boundaries of the Punjab were extended. Although the British were taking over most of India at this time, they did not try to take over the Punjab while Maharajah Ranjit Singh was in charge of his army, which now fought with cannons as well as with swords.

Pain and division

When Maharajah Ranjit Singh died in 1839, there was no one who could command the Sikh army in such a firm and competent way. The army became less organized, and when the British fought the Sikh army in 1846, the Sikhs were eventually forced to surrender. The British then took over part of the Punjab. Three years later, the British army and the Sikhs fought again. Although the Sikhs fought bravely and came close to winning, the British at last took over complete rule of the Punjab, but they realized what good soldiers the Sikhs were. Later, many Sikhs fought in the British armed forces in both World Wars.

After World War I, trouble began again between the British and the Sikhs, leading to a massacre of Sikhs at Amritsar in 1919. The British began to lose control of India. There were also clashes between Hindus, Muslims and Sikhs. Finally, in 1947, India was divided and part of it became Pakistan, a new country under Muslim rulership. Pakistan included part of the Punjab, and many Sikhs moved from their homes into India. Sikhs had hoped for their own homeland. Many still hope for this, but today Sikhs in India are part of the

Indian state, in which all religions are given the same respect.

In the Punjab today

Sikh beliefs have stayed basically the same through all these events, although there have been some groups of Sikhs who wanted changes in the way that their religion was practiced.

Sikhs in the Punjab now work at a variety of jobs – some traditional, such as farming, and some more modern: many Sikhs are involved in transport, driving taxis and freight trucks. Most Sikhs have no problems in adjusting to the modern world while keeping their beliefs.

Above: Many Sikhs believe that they should have their own independent state, which they will call Khalistan. The people in this photograph are showing their respect for those who have died fighting for such an independent Sikh state. They are displaying a sword in their hands as a symbol of freedom.

39

Sikhs in the world

Although Sikhism began in the Punjab, it has now spread to many parts of the world. Most Sikhs who have left their homeland have done so during the 20th century, because travel has become easier, cheaper and safer.

Moving with the army

Sikhs moved first to other parts of India, although the number of Sikhs in the rest of India has always been small compared with the number in the Punjab. When the British finally defeated the Sikhs and took control of the Punjab, they recruited Sikhs into the British army.

These Sikh soldiers traveled around the world, and some of them decided to settle down in the countries they had visited. Many Sikhs left the Punjab for only a few years. They sent money home to help their families, and later went back to join them. Others decided to stay abroad permanently, and saved up their money, so that their families could come and join them in their new countries.

There were several reasons for these Sikhs to leave India. Some left because they were interested in going to new places. Others left because they were looking for a better standard of living. They found that in other countries they could earn as much for a few months' work as they could earn in a year in India. Their families would also get a better education.

Finding new homes

In 1947, many Sikhs had another reason to leave the Punjab. The British gave up their rule over India, and the country was divided into two parts, India and Pakistan. Many Sikhs who had lived in the part of the Punjab which was now in Pakistan decided to leave India altogether. They set off to make new lives for themselves.

Many of the Sikhs who left India moved to Britain. In fact, more Sikhs live in Britain than in any other country except India. Sikhs have settled in most of the major cities in Britain, including London, Birmingham, Manchester, Cardiff and Glasgow. Some British Sikhs arrived at the beginning of the 20th century. Others came later, often as traveling salesmen, and stayed on during World War II, either helping in ammunition factories or joining the army. A great many arrived after the partition of India. They chose to settle in the big cities because there was plenty of work available; at the time there was very little unemployment in Britain's large cities.

The New World

Many Sikhs have moved to the United States and to Canada. The first of these arrived before World War I, but in 1917 the Americans passed a law which prevented Sikhs, as well as many other people, from becoming American citizens. In 1946 a new bill was passed by the American Congress which allowed some Sikhs to become American citizens.

Sikhs who went to America settled first in California, where they were able to use their farming skills. Some of these Sikhs moved east, and there are now fairly large Sikh communities in New York, Washington and Chicago. Many white people and black people of Afro-Caribbean origin have recently become Sikhs, especially in New York.

Wherever Sikhs have settled, they have tended to work in particular occupations.

Below: Even when Sikhs have left India and made their homes in other countries, they usually keep in touch through relatives who still live in India. Those who can afford to do so often return for visits.

This Sikh woman lives in Britain, but keeps in touch with her family in India by mail. The letter she is reading has been written in Gurmukhi, the Punjabi script.

ਸੱਚਾ ਅਮਰ ਗੋਬਿੰਦ ਦਾ, ਸੁਣ ਗੁਰ ਪਿਆਰੇ। ਸਤਿ ਸੰਗਤਿ ਮੇਲਾਪ ੩, ਪੰਚ ਦੂਤ ਸੰਘਾਰੇ।   ੳ ਗੁਰੂ ਗੋਬਿੰਦ ਹੁਇ ਪ੍ਰਗਟਿਆ ਦਸਵੇ ਅਵਤਾਰਾ। ਜਿ

Sikhs often join the police force or the army. In India Sikhs have traditionally been involved in transportation, and when they emigrate they often find jobs working on the railways or buses. More educated Sikhs can be found in professional jobs, such as medicine or the law.

Changes and challenges

When Sikhs move to a new country, they sometimes find that they have problems there. Some of these problems are caused by the attitudes of other people. Some people are racially prejudiced: they do not like people who come from a different culture, especially those whose skin is a different color from their own. These people are only a minority, but their dislike makes it difficult for Sikhs and other immigrants to settle down happily in their new country.

Another problem for Sikhs outside India is that they feel there is a danger they might lose their culture and traditions. Many of the young Sikhs outside India may never have seen India, and speak very little Punjabi. It is very important for Sikhs to feel at home in their country, but they also believe it is vital to keep their own culture and religion.

Above: There is a large model of the Golden Temple next to the *takht* (or throne) in which the Guru Granth Sahib rests in the Khalsa Diwan Society gurdwara in Vancouver. Many Sikhs moved to Canada after 1953 when the Canadian government made it easier to go and settle there.

Left: These Kenyan Sikhs are carrying the Guru Granth Sahib in a triumphal procession at the opening of a new gurdwara. Sikhs who had been in the British Army settled in countries such as Singapore, Malaysia and Kenya. Many of those who went to East Africa worked on the railways.

41

Further information

A glossary of useful words

Adi Granth "first book." The name given to the collection of hymns put together by Guru Arjan which formed the basis of the Sikh holy book.

amrit "nectar." A drink made from sugar crystals dissolved in water and stirred with a sword.

Anand Sahib a Sikh hymn used at all services.

Ardas the prayer which is said at the end of the main part of all Sikh services.

Asa da Vaar the hymn sung at the beginning of every service in the gurdwara.

Baisakhi a Sikh festival in April which celebrates the founding of the Khalsa.

Bhai "brother." A title of respect used by the Sikhs for people whom they honor.

caste a system by which Hindus divide society into groups according to birth.

channani the canopy over the Guru Granth Sahib.

chatka the Sikh way of killing animals for food. Sikhs should not eat meat which has been killed in a way which causes the animal unnecessary suffering.

chunni a scarf often worn by Sikh women.

cremated burned; Sikhs do not bury the dead. Instead they cremate or burn the bodies on a very hot fire.

Diwali a festival held in either October or November when Sikhs remember the release of Guru Hargobind from prison.

granthi the name given to the person who reads from the Guru Granth Sahib at the gurdwara.

gurdwara "the door of the Guru." The Sikh place of worship.

Gurmukhi "the Guru's word." The written form of Punjabi. The Sikh holy book, the Guru Granth Sahib, is written in this alphabet.

gurpurb a festival celebrating the birth of one of the Gurus, or remembering his martyrdom.

Guru "teacher." The title given to the ten great human teachers of Sikhism and to the Sikh holy book.

Guru Granth Sahib the holy book of Sikhism, containing hymns written by the Gurus as well as hymns by Hindu and Muslim writers. The book is treated with the same respect given to the human Gurus.

gutkha a small personal copy of extracts from the Guru Granth Sahib. The *gutkha*, too, must be treated with respect.

Harimandir "house of God." The temple at Amritsar, built by the fifth Guru.

Hola Mohalla a festival held in either February or March when Sikhs gather for mock battles and competitions of skill.

Japji Sahib the Sikh morning prayer.

the five K.'s five symbols whose names in Punjabi all begin with "k." They are worn by Sikhs, especially those who have joined the Khalsa.

kaccha loose shorts worn by Sikhs as underclothes; one of the five K.'s.

kanga a comb: one of the five K.'s.

kara a steel bracelet worn on the right wrist; one of the five K.'s.

karah parshad a sweet dish made of flour, butter, sugar and water which is shared at the end of the main part of Sikh services.

Kaur "princess," the last name given to all Sikh women.

kesh uncut hair; one of the five K.'s. The *kesh* includes the beard, which should not be trimmed or shaved.

Khalsa the brotherhood of Sikhs, founded by the tenth Guru, Guru Gobind Singh.

khanda the double-edged sword which is often used as a symbol of Sikhism.

kirpan sword; one of the five K.'s. Nowadays usually carried in the form of a small knife, or a knife symbol set into the *kanga* or comb.

Kirtan the singing of hymns. All the hymns which Sikhs sing are verses from the Guru Granth Sahib.

langar "free kitchen." All gurdwaras have a dining hall which is open to all, and where everyone can sit down and eat together.

Manji Sahib the cushion on which the Guru Granth Sahib rests when it is being read.

martyr a person who is killed because of their religious beliefs.

meditation thinking quietly and deeply about God.

Mool Mantra the first hymn composed by Guru Nanak, which sums up Sikh belief.

nadar "grace;" the word Sikhs use to describe God's taking special notice of a person.

pala a piece of material used to tie the bride and groom together while they take part in the Sikh wedding ceremony.

panj pyares "the five beloved." The name given to the five Sikhs who were prepared to give their lives for their faith.

patkha a piece of cloth with which young Sikh boys cover their hair until they learn to tie the turban.

Punjab "five rivers." A northern region of India which is the homeland of Sikhism.

Rahiras a prayer said at the end of the day to thank God for the successes of the day.

rumala the cloth which is wrapped around the Guru Granth Sahib.

Sat Guru "true Guru;" one of the names which Sikhs use for God.

sewa service to others. One of the most important parts of Sikh belief.

sewadar a name given to anyone who is performing *sewa*.

shalwar baggy trousers often worn with a long tunic (kameez) by Sikh women.

Singh "lion;" the last name given to all Sikh men.

Sohila Mahala the prayer which Sikhs say every evening.

takht a seat of authority. The four *takhts* are the places where all important decisions about Sikh beliefs and practices are made.

turban the distinctive headgear worn by Sikhs. It is made from a long piece of cloth.

Waheguru "wonderful Lord." One of the Sikh names for God.

The ten Gurus

GURU NANAK (1469–1539)

GURU ANGAD (1539–1552)

GURU AMAR DAS (1552–1574)

GURU RAM DAS (1574–1581)

GURU ARJAN (1581–1606)

GURU HARGOBIND (1606–1644)

GURU HAR RAI (1644–1661)

GURU HAR KRISHAN (1661–1664)

GURU TEGH BAHADUR (1664–1675)

GURU GOBIND SINGH (1675–1708)

The Sikh calendar

As well as the three main festivals which have already been described, Sikhs celebrate many other festivals known as *gurpurbs*. These are held to help Sikhs to remember events in the lives of the Gurus. Some of these festivals are celebrated all over the world, while others are only celebrated in the area where the event took place.

At the festivals, the Guru Granth Sahib is often read through from beginning to end. In India the holy book is usually carried through the streets in a procession. Competitions are held, special speakers are brought in to give lectures and everyone eats at a *langar*. Here is a list of the main festivals, beginning with Baisakhi, the Sikh New Year:

APRIL 13th	– Baisakhi
APRIL	– Birthday of the 9th Guru, Guru Tegh Bahadur – Birthday of the 5th Guru, Guru Arjan
MAY	– Birthday of the 2nd Guru, Guru Angad – Birthday of the 3rd Guru, Guru Amar Das
MAY-JUNE	– Martyrdom of Guru Arjan
JUNE	– Birthday of the 6th Guru, Guru Hargobind
JULY	– Birthday of the 8th Guru, Guru Har Krishan
OCTOBER-NOVEMBER	– Diwali
NOVEMBER	– The birthday of Guru Nanak
DECEMBER/JANUARY	– The birthday of Guru Gobind Singh – Martyrdom of Guru Tegh Bahadur
FEBRUARY-MARCH	– Hola Mohalla

Books for further reading

For children
Sikhism by W. Owen Cole and Piara Singh
Sambhi (International Pubns. Service, 1977)
Stories from Sikh History (Ten Volumes) by ·
Kartar Singh and Gurdial S. Dhillon
(Auromere Inc., 1971)
The Story of Guru Nanak by Mala Singh
(Auromere Inc., 1979)

For teachers
The Sikhs: Their Religious Beliefs and Practices
by W. Owen Cole and Piara S. Sambhi
(Routledge and Kegan, 1978)
The Sikh Gurus by Kartar Duggal (Advent
Books, 1980)
Sunset of the Sikh Empire by Sita Ram Kohli
(Associated Faculty Press, 1967)
Sikhism by Daljeet Singh (Orient Book
Distributors, 1979)
Guru Gobind Singh by Gopal Singh
(Auromere, Inc., 1979)
The Heritage of the Sikhs by Harbans Singh
(South Asia Books, 1983)
The Sikh Revolution by Jagjit Singh
(Humanities Press, 1981)
The Sikhs Today by Khushwant Singh (South
Asia Books, 1976)

Visiting a gurdwara

If you wish to visit a gurdwara, you may need
to find out which is the nearest to where you
live. You will be able to find out the address of
your nearest gurdwara from you local library.
There are gurdwaras in many major cities.

Most gurdwaras are happy to welcome
visitors, but if you are going in a large group,
you should contact the gurdwara first and let
them know when you wish to visit them.

The main service is usually held on a
Sunday. It usually begins quite early, but it is
quite usual for people to arrive part of the
way through. Unless you understand Punjabi
it is best to arrive some time after the service
has begun, as it will go on for several hours.

All visitors to the gurdwara must take off
their shoes and cover their heads before they
enter the room which contains the Guru
Granth Sahib. Gurdwaras often provide
head-coverings for visitors, but your own hat,
scarf or clean handkerchief will be acceptable.

At the end of the service, *karah parshad*
will be passed around; it is a sweet, sticky
food which will be placed in your hands;
napkins are usually provided to wipe your
hands afterwards. After this you will go to
another room to share in the *langar*. Men and
women usually sit apart, but this is a custom,
not a rule. Food is eaten by being scooped up
by hand with kinds of bread called chappati
and roti.

Index

Numbers in heavy type refer to picture captions, or to the pictures themselves.

Illustration Credits
Key to position of illustrations:
(T) top, (L) left, (B) bottom, (R) right

Artists
Julia Osorno: 11, 15, 20–21
Raymond Turvey: 25, 38

Photographic sources
Camerapix Hutchison Library: 30, 31B, 41B
Cam Culbert: 8, 22, 23B 27T, 27B, 28, 33T, 41T
W. Owen Cole: 26, 29T, 29B
Daily Telegraph Colour Library: contents page, 9
Douglas Dickens: 37
Format/Sarita Sharma: 40
Sally and Richard Greenhill: 24
J. Kalidas: 19
Christine Osborne: 11, 15, 16, 32, 34B, 39T
Bury Peerless: cover, endpapers, title page, 8–9, 12, 13, 17, 31T, 33B, 34T, 35
Raghu Rai, 'The Sikhs', Lustre Press Pvt. Ltd.: 18L
David Richardson: 10, 14, 23T, 36T, 36B
Rex Features: 18R, 39B

1 2 3 4 5 6 7 8 9 10—U—93 92 91 90 89 88 87 86 85